wylde women

wylde women

in celebration of the feminine...

- terri st.cloud

bone sigh books

ISBN: 978-0-9815440-3-8 (pbk)
bone sigh arts
www.bonesigharts.com
www.bonesighbooks.com

the 'i am' stone on our cover
was created by fre bracy.

cover art: yohan
www.bfg-productions.com

book layout / design:
zakk and yo
www.mazuzu.com

contents

contents

there's a woman who came along
and touched my soul
like no other.

to me,
she embodies the wylde.

she's not just strong,
she's strong all the way to her bones.
she's not just wise,
she's the silly kinda wise where she can laugh in the
middle of the hardest moments.
she's not just gentle,
she's the firm kinda gentle,
loving you into what you have the potential to be.
she's courageous and brave
and beautiful and stunning.
her eyes knock your soul over ...
colored with compassion and love,
the deep kind that's learned thru life's sorrows.

thru those sick-to-your-stomach-scary times
where we just held on tight to each other,
to the ridiculous silly times
where we laughed til we cried,
she taught me how to open and live more fully.
from the first moment she came into my life,
she came offering her heart.
and her heart touched me
and changed me.

she is one of the most amazing women
i have ever had the privilege to grow with...

and it is to her and her spirit
i would like to dedicate this book.

fre, this book is yours.

Some years back, i did my first joint art show with several other women artists. we called the show 'when wylde women dream' and we began calling ourselves 'the wylde women.'

we were just a small group of local artists doing local shows together. in all honesty, we weren't very impressive. but it didn't seem to matter. women showed up at the events intrigued with the name of the group. women were looking for the feminine. they wanted support, encouragement, freedom to be creative and to express themselves......they wanted wylde.

it was for that first art show that i put together a home-made book called 'bone sighs, the wylde women edition.' much to my delight, it became a hit! this volume is a spin off of that first home-made version.

it's been a lot of traveling down my own personal journey since those days. i've shared with many different women along the way and i've fallen in love with the feminine.

women are amazing creatures, full of wisdom and compassion and strength and ingenuity. i like to think of all those things as 'the wylde.' we all have the wylde inside of us. i forget that sometimes and need to be reminded. a certain word, a certain phrase can bring me back to remembering. sometimes a friend who knows. sometimes looking at the sky will do it. whatever brings me back, i'm always grateful to return...and i wonder how i could have left
in the first place!

it is my deepest hope that something in this book can be a reminder for you...that it somehow can grab your hand and pull you back when you need it...and that you too will land back where you started from and wonder how it was you ever left it!

the feminine is a gift. may we hold it and honor it and let it lead us into the wylde. and once there, may we offer that wylde to the world.

the dance of the wylde

she danced the dance
of the daring and the trusting ~
and to her delight...
magic showed up!

me, myself

i commit to me, myself, today.
i vow to listen to and follow and believe
in my goodness.
to recognize my strength
and wield it with the added power of compassion.
to know my heart
and trust it and not turn to outside expectations
to feed it, but rather turn to my own inner guidance
to lead me.
to know that i am the woman i want to be
and work to uncover more of my beauty daily.
and to be gentle with myself when
i slip - loving myself even in the darkness.
to me, myself, i give my love.
and it is from me, myself, my love is returned.

her circle

some believed in her.
others did not.
she joined the circle of believers
and rejoiced with them.

my heart

i took my heart back and made it mine.
it hurt at first....
and then it sang.

three friends

they sat around the table mixing hope and wisdom
with their tears.
each about to start a different journey.
each at a different place on the road...
and yet somehow each at the same place.

strings

slowly she started pulling the strings off.
and then faster and faster...
she couldn't get them off fast enough!
until finally -
"ahhhhhhhhhh" she gasped ~
freedom!

stepping forward

what she lost wasn't healthy.
what she gained was.

delight

she wanted to honor the wise one
inside herself but didn't know how.
the answer echoed from her depths ~
see who you are.
become more of who you are.
delight in your soul.

fitting in

it saddened her at first.
she didn't fit in.
she had never fit in.
she didn't think she ever would.
but then, slowly, the smile came...
and grew.
she fit in with herself now.
for the first time she had grown
into herself and fit.
and that was enough.

mantra

i will not allow myself to
be less than i am
to meet anybody's
expectations.

her truth

speaking her truth got easier and easier
once she believed in herself.
and the more she spoke, the more she believed.
and the more she believed, the more her spirit shone.
there was no stopping her now ~
she was ready to dazzle the world with her light.

her power

she took her power back ~
without permission.

black sheep

she's a black sheep with a blue moon on her back.

rains

with the rains came her madness -
and she floated away.

the first notes

hearing the first notes inside herself,
her eyes got wide.
growing louder and stronger,
colors began mixing with the sounds.
holding on tight and letting go all at once,
she stepped back into the dance.

souls

she didn't just survive -
she became.

giving

maybe when you really love yourself
you can see beyond that self -
and then maybe you never give yourself away.
maybe you just give.

growth

like the rings of a tree
marking its growth,
the ripples of honesty that
circled thru her life,
marked hers.

she fell

she fell from their graces
into her truth.

one's self

in the love of one's self
the connections of all the universe are felt
and one's flame burns pure.

the music roared

the good girl...
the girl they approved of
had evolved.
she was now the woman
living real.
the woman they couldn't
box.
she danced.
they stared.
and the music roared.

somehow

it's entirely up to me," she thought.
terror filled her.
but she'd do it anyway.
because somehow she could.

the door closed

they almost took her once.
it wasn't going to happen again.
the door closed.
and she moved on.

choices

she would sacrifice what she had to
to go where she needed.

magic

magic showed up again and again.
she learned to look for it,
recognize it and
delight in it.

free hands

setting her empty bucket down,
she turned towards her joy.
now she had both hands
free to grasp it.

becoming

it wasn't that she was growing and changing, was it?
it was that she was finally allowing herself to become.

her answer

one day her answer wandered in
and took her breath away.

and the universe listened....

the universe listened.
she listened.
and the dance that had been quiet
for so long inside of her
began again.

mad intensities

mad intensities don't just happen she said -
they consume you in a moment,
but they grow from lifetimes ago.

acceptance

it finally occurred to her -
accepting others didn't mean
shutting down her true feelings
towards them -
it meant accepting her reaction to them
as much as accepting them!
it meant accepting her feelings as well!
this changed everything -
she inhaled the long forgotten feeling
of freedom and began again.

from the stars

she brought it with her from the stars.
and after she spread some of its light,
she would bring it back.
because now she knew.

beyond her

it was beyond her and she knew it.
she knelt down in its intensity.
gratitude filled her,
tears cleansed her
and energy flowed thru her.

awakening

and she loved again…

i'm scared

"i'm scared," she realized, running to her room.
"ooh, i'm scared," she mumbled, covering her head.
"i'm so scared," she cried, reaching for her friends.
"i'm tiny and i'm scared," she trembled, knowing it was her's to hold.
"yes, i am scared," she spoke, turning in its direction.
"i am scared and i am here," she shouted staring in its eyes.
the eyes stared back...
and loved her.

colors

shakily at first, her belief opened her world.
steadier, that belief changed her world.
solid now, it colored her world, her life and her soul.

waking up

it's a powerful thing to watch a woman wake up.

girlfriends

she told her her secrets
and secrets were returned,
and they laughed at how alike they were.
she whispered her fears,
and fears were whispered back,
and they cried over how hurt they were.
she confessed her dreams
and dreams were confessed back,
and they danced at the possibilities they were.

new keys

the new door wouldn't open
with the old key –
she found scrubbing the key
wasn't enough.

she needed a brand new one.

perhaps

perhaps power is letting go of the grip of the past
and standing empty handed facing the
future.

freedom

it was in accepting them
and knowing herself,
she found freedom.

not her deal

it wasn't her deal,
it was their's, she thought.
only this time, those weren't just
words to help her detach.
she was detached.
it was truth.
and she danced with delight in her
freedom.

ecstasy

she had lost a life time of things
and felt sadness
until she stared at the magic
she had found
and felt ecstasy

trade?

would you trade what you have found
for what you have lost? she asked herself.
the tears poured down her face.
no! she screamed,
her being shaking from the sound.
for she had found her heart, she had
found real -
she had found life.

becoming love

slowly, she was beginning to see it,
it wasn't about acting or thinking
or getting or giving love.
it was about breathing love,
living love –
becoming love.

the flood

the flood was knocking and she knew it.
opening the door, she released her grasp
and stepped aside.
the trickle flowed in slowly at first.
then stronger and stronger the current
picked up. pulling her under,
carrying her with it, she lost herself
and became the water.

languages

the language of boxes
and boundaries and borders
that her mind spoke made no
sense to her heart.
silencing those thoughts,
she allowed her heart to sing
and let her spirit dance.

she flew

having tired of the negative words –
she laid them down.
being finished with the weighted boots,
she burned them.
touching a feather to her tears,
she slipped on her wings,
turned to her sky –
and flew.

kindness

understanding now that his was
the way to open her heart,
she dropped to her knees
and opened herself
to its presence.

solitary flight

the solitary flight
brings unimagined strength
and opens the heavens.

headin' for the cells

do you really think we can change at
a cellular level? she asked.
that'd be a lot of work, she said.
taking my hand in hers, she grinned.
c'mon! we're headin' for the cells!

live and laugh

live and dance and laugh,
being free with your heart.
for there is enough always –
even when you forget.

the mud puddle

the mud puddle was back there.
exactly where she had left it.
it wouldn't move.
for that was the nature of mud puddles.
but she would,
for that was the nature of her.

in the right direction

and she turned back to where she
had been heading in the first place –
knowing it was beyond okay.
knowing it was right.
knowing it was home.

you will know

they can't tell you when you'll know.
they can't tell you how you'll know.
you just need to hold on to the fact
that you will know.

missed opportunities

"missed opportunities" he said.
he had missed another.
how many had she missed,
she wondered.
it was up to her to grab the moments-
and she would.

miracles

she danced
and laughed
and threw back
her head,
exclaiming, "it's a miracle!"
finally, tiring herself out –
she quietly gave thanks.

radically accept

radically accept release.
wildly desperately let go.
quietly hear the inner calm.
slowly, begin to know.

possibilities

knowing she had to let go-
she released her grasp.
massaging her fingers,
she reached for the possibilities
ahead of her.

ever new

maybe the holding stunts you,
she thought.
maybe growth is release,
non gripping, flowing,
ever forward, ever motion,
ever new…

meeting herself

she cut her hair, knowing she
was really cutting the cord.
she changed her clothes,
knowing she was really changing
her beliefs.
she grabbed her keys,
knowing she was really grabbing her
life.
she said goodbye,
knowing she was really meeting
herself for the first time.

two worlds

she wasn't them.
she couldn't be.
was she going to claim
herself as herself or
forever be half way between worlds?

dancing on air

if you live between two worlds,
trying to please them all.........you
eventually snap.
if you jump into your own world,
trying to listen to your heart...
you eventually dance on air.

you

it's your thoughts and your spirit and your
creativity and your flair and your heart
and your sparkle and your passion and your
loves and your courage that make up the
incredible mix of who you are...
why oh why do we let others tell us what
our mix should be??

happy

i can't make you happy. only you can do that.
you can't make me happy. only i can do that.
i'll make me happy. you make you happy.
and maybe we can dance together from time
to time.........

steps

she had touched it.
now she wanted to live it.
seemed maybe the first step
was acceptance,
and the second step,
laughter.

continuing on

almost crumbling to the ground,
she stopped. looking at how far she had traveled
and all it had taken to get there,
she recognized her strength.
the strengths she had inside of her,
the strength she had gained along the way ~
her inner power.
and so,
she stood up.
standing tall,
she faced forward
and continued on.

a vow to my heart

i will work on the act of listening to you
and my listening abilities will grow.
i will honor those things you relay
to me and act upon them.
when i act upon them,
i will know that i am living my truth
and owe no explanations to anyone.
i will believe in your ability to accept all emotions
and will not close down to protect you.
i will direct my energies and my power
to places that will strengthen you, not deplete you.
i will follow you in the way i wish the world would follow you.
the child of the universe and the heart
shall meld and we shall dance as one.

not knowing

not knowing what her heart felt,
she dumped her beliefs all over the floor.
before she could sort thru them,
the strong ones leaped right back
into her hands.

maybe it's time

maybe it's time to take care of yourself.
maybe it's time to scream out loud
that you don't have the answers
and you just plain can't figure out what
it's all about...
but you're in this for the full ride.
maybe it's time to stop doin' the half ride.
maybe it's time to step into it all.
to weep your guts out.
to hurt all the way to your core.
to allow that hurt to be there.
maybe it's time to embrace the love
and believe in it even tho it's not always perfect...
but it is always right.
maybe it's time to shout out to your depths
that you do matter
and you will do all in your power to live healthy.
maybe it's time to stop just getting thru,
just surviving.
maybe it's time to grab the gift you've been given
and celebrate every single piece of it -
including the pain that brought you here.
maybe it's time.

forget the maybe....and know it...
it is time.

her core

reaching down past her depths,
she touched her fingers to her core.
wrapping her hands around its pulse,
she became the beat of her soul.

bold as love

"bold as love," he sang -
and she knew she wanted to be.

terri didn't know she was a writer, didn't know she was an artist, she ji plain ol' didn't know a heck of a lot of anything. and then some good oi fashioned, gut wrenching, heart ripping pain gripped her life, and she started to discover things about herself. she began her journey inward. when the pain got to be too much for her, she spilled out her feelings on paper. wanting to honor those feelings somehow, she added art to them. it was with that mixing of spilling and honoring that bone sighs were born.

needing to find a way to support herself and her sons, she began peddling her watercolor bone sighs shop to shop. thru an amazing journey of tears, miracles, trust, terror, laughter, squeezing her eyes closed tight, and following her heart, somehow bone sigh arts became a real business.

home-made books were offered for awhile among her prints and cards. cumbersome to make and lacking the desired quality, there came a time when the books needed to become "real." grabbing her sons, terri and the guys decided to go into print!

without terri's sons, bone sigh arts/books would never ever have become what it has. funny how the very reason for the business became what made the business successful. those boys are everything to both terri and bone sighs!

josh is the oldest. an old soul musician, born entertainer, and a loveable guy! yo yo is their gentle giant who's turning into the world's best graphic designer! and zakk is the logical one. computer geek and mad inventor with the marshmallow heart.

and! the boys have expanded into beginning their own businesses for themselves! (check out the information page for a listing of their websites!)

it's been quite a journey for them all.

terri's still scratchin' her head wonderin' if she'll ever figure any of it out! probably not....but she'll keep trying anyway!

- *info* -

terri st.cloud
15809 menk rd
accokeek md 20607
granolastew@gmail.com

bone sigh arts
BoneSighArts.com

bone sigh books
BoneSighBooks.com

Zakk and Yo's business
Mazuzu.com

Yohan's business
BFG-Productions.com

Josh's business
Poodleman.com

Breinigsville, PA USA
28 October 2010
248198BV00005B/2/P